For my kids,
I love you to the moon and back (plus SO MUCH MORE)!!!

For my mom crew,
Thank you for the laughter, support, and sanity.

For my family,
Thank you for being the BEST babysitters; these kids are *so* lucky
to have you.

For my husband,
Thank you for making this all possible; you're our everything.

/ / /

My mom is a lawyer.

After high school, she went to school for an extra seven years.

She had to read a lot of very heavy books
with very big words.

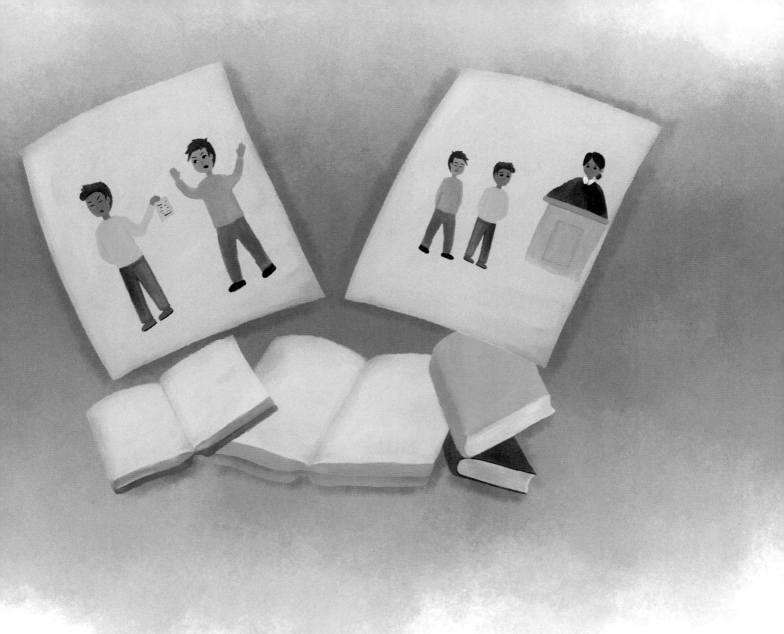

Most of the books were about cases. Cases are real-life stories about people's disagreements.
In every case, rules are made for the rest of us to follow.

In law school, she learned how to speak so people would listen.

She learned how to write so people would understand.

She learned how to help people and keep our world safe.

After law school, she had to pass a very hard test in order to practice law.

Even now, she has to take more classes every year
so she can understand how new laws work.

There are many kinds of lawyers.
Some lawyers help people when they are hurt.

Some lawyers put people in "time out"
    when they break the rules.

Some lawyers protect people who are unfairly accused.

Some lawyers help businesses.

Some lawyers help people buy and sell their property.

Some lawyers protect our earth, our culture, and our lives.

Lawyers help make laws. Laws are rules that protect us -
like for kids to wear their seatbelts so they can be safe.

Laws are there so people won't hit each other, or take things that don't belong to them, or say things that aren't true.

Lawyers make sure that laws are applied fairly to everyone.

When my mom works from home, I hear her say words like, "exhibits," "stipulations," and "evidence."

One thing my mom always says is that *words have power.*

Sometimes my mom works late, and I miss her.
I know she misses me too and loves me very much.

Even though my mom is a lawyer, she's just like other moms. She makes me dinner, reads me books, and always kisses me goodnight.

I am proud of my mom for being a lawyer.

She is making the world a better place.

This book was a collaboration between two working moms
on opposite ends of the world - California and Pakistan.

Many late nights, weekends, and hundreds of messages
created the details captured within these pages.

Made in the USA
Las Vegas, NV
14 February 2024

My Mom is a Lawyer is the first in a series
of children's books that help explain what
a child's professional mom does for a living,
and how she is making the world a better place.

Written by a lawyer mom
for other lawyer moms.

ni
BOOKS

ISBN 9781737168706

90000

9 781737 168706

Danielle L. Forbes   Anastasiia Bielik

BIG THINGS:
Mommy's C-Section Recovery